Bridging Divides: Navigating Hindu-Muslim Relations in Contemporary India

Ankush vig

Published by Ankush vig, 2024.

BRIDGING DIVIDES: NAVIGATING HINDU-MUSLIM RELATIONS IN CONTEMPORARY INDIA

First edition. May 4, 2024.

ISBN: 979-8215965573

Written by Ankush vig.

Also by Ankush vig

Equity Endeavours: A Pioneering Path to Profitable Investing
Ayodhya Unveiled: A History of Faith, Struggle and Triumph
BJP Unboxed: The Story of India's Political Powerhouse
Navigating Relationships: A Guide to Healthy Choices and Happiness
Bridging Divides: Navigating Hindu-Muslim Relations in Contemporary India

Table of Contents

Conclusion:

- Emerging Themes and Insights
- The Ongoing Narrative of Hindu-Muslim Relations
- Lessons Learned and Future Considerations

Introduction:

India, a land of myriad cultures, languages, and religions, has stood as a testament to the rich tapestry of human diversity for centuries. Among its numerous religious communities, Hindus and Muslims constitute two of the largest, contributing significantly to the socio-cultural fabric of the nation. The coexistence of these communities has been both a source of strength and, at times, a site of tension and conflict. "Bridging Divides" seeks to explore the nuanced dynamics of Hindu-Muslim relations in contemporary India, unravelling the historical, social, and political intricacies that have shaped their interaction.

- **Diversity as a Strength**

India's strength lies in its diversity, a kaleidoscope of traditions, beliefs, and practices that have evolved over millennia. Hindus, with their pantheon of deities, sacred texts, and diverse rituals, share this vast subcontinent with Muslims, adherents to the monotheistic faith of Islam. The interweaving of these distinct cultural and religious narratives has created a pluralistic society that, for much of its history, has managed to find harmony in diversity.

The Indian subcontinent has been a crucible of ideas, with the confluence of Hindu and Islamic influences leading to the synthesis of unique art, architecture, and philosophical thought. From the Mughal monuments that stand as testaments to architectural grandeur to the philosophical exchanges between Sufi saints and Hindu mystics, the shared history of these communities is one marked by both cooperation and contestation.

- **Historical Perspectives**

However, this harmony has not always prevailed. "Bridging Divides" delves into the historical dimensions of Hindu-Muslim relations, examining pivotal events that have shaped the contours of the present-day discourse. The destruction of Hindu temples, the burning of universities and libraries, and the imposition of discriminatory taxes on non-Muslims are chapters in the historical narrative that have left indelible marks on the psyche of both communities.

The creation of Pakistan in 1947, carving out a separate nation based on religious lines, was a watershed moment that altered the demographic landscape and sowed the seeds of new challenges. The partition, while addressing immediate political concerns, ushered in an era of religious animosity and migration, leaving scars that linger even today. "Bridging Divides" aims to unravel the complexities of these historical events and their lasting impact on the relations between Hindus and Muslims.

Contemporary Challenges

As we step into the present, contemporary challenges come to the forefront. Extremism, political polarisation, and divisive ideologies have exacerbated tensions, leading to periodic outbreaks of violence and social discord. The influence of political movements, every party has played a significant role in shaping public discourse and framing the narratives of identity and belonging.

Religious practices and theological differences, such as the disdain for idol worship and polytheism, further contribute to the intricate web of challenges. Questions surrounding the implementation of Sharia over court, the coexistence of diverse legal systems, and the pursuit of a Uniform Civil Code underscore the ongoing dialogue on the balance between religious freedoms and the imperatives of a secular state.

- **Government Initiatives: A New Dawn**

"Bridging Divides" turns its focus towards the proactive measures taken by the government to address the challenges at hand. The chapters on government initiatives highlight policies aimed at socio economic upliftment, education, and infrastructure development. The book examines the efforts made by the Modi government to provide jobs, business opportunities, healthcare, and education, with a particular emphasis on the inclusion of minority communities.

Drawing inspiration from successful models like Singapore, the book explores techniques for fostering religious harmony through interfaith dialogue, education, and inclusive policies. It examines the role of nationalism, both as a unifying force and a potential source of division, in shaping the government's approach to communal relations.

Chapter 1: Destruction of Hindu Temples

The ancient echoes of India's religious landscape carry the whispers of countless tales, the harmonious symphony of diverse beliefs, practices, and sacred spaces. Yet, woven into this rich tapestry is a narrative marked by periods of turbulence and discord. Among the most poignant chapters in this story is the destruction of Hindu temples, a historical phenomenon that has left an indelible mark on the collective memory of the nation.

- **The Mosaic of Temples**

India, with its vibrant cultural and religious heritage, boasts an abundance of temples, each a testament to centuries of devotion, artistry, and spiritual expression. From the grandeur of the Khajuraho temples to the intricate carvings of the Ellora caves, these sacred spaces have stood as embodiments of faith, attracting pilgrims, scholars, and admirers from across the globe.

However, the pages of history also bear witness to a darker side, where many temples faced desecration and destruction. The motives behind such actions varied, ranging from political conquests to religious zealotry, leaving a trail of shattered stones and broken sculptures in their wake.

- **Historical Context**

The destruction of Hindu temples can be traced back to various periods in history, each marked by its unique set of circumstances. One of the earliest instances occurred during the invasions by Mahmud of Ghazni in the 11th century. Mahmud, driven by a combination of political ambition and religious fervour, targeted Hindu temples in the Indian subcontinent.

The Somnath Temple, dedicated to Lord Shiva, stands as a poignant symbol of Mahmud's incursions. The repeated sackings of Somnath in the 11th century resulted in the looting and destruction of the temple, illustrating the intersection of political power and religious animosity.

- **Political Conquests and Cultural Consequences**

The mediaeval period witnessed further instances of temple destruction, often intertwined with the dynamics of political conquest. The Delhi Sultanate and later the Mughal Empire, while contributing significantly to India's cultural synthesis, were also responsible for the destruction of certain Hindu temples.

The destruction of the Kesava Deo Temple in Mathura during the reign of Aurangzeb remains a stark reminder of this turbulent era. The temple, believed to be the birthplace of Lord Krishna, faced systematic desecration and eventual demolition, reflecting the complex interplay between political power and religious identity.

- **Symbolic Connotations**

The destruction of Hindu temples went beyond mere acts of vandalism; it carried profound symbolic connotations. Temples, with their intricate architecture and revered deities, were not only centres of worship but also repositories of cultural and artistic expression. The desecration of these sacred spaces sought to undermine the very foundations of the communities they served.

The symbolic nature of temple destruction extended beyond the physical realm. It aimed to erode the cultural identity of the communities associated with these places of worship, fostering a sense of vulnerability and subjugation.

- **Impact on Hindu-Muslim Relations**

The repercussions of temple destruction resonate through the annals of history, shaping the contours of Hindu-Muslim relations. While these actions were often driven by political motives, they fueled a narrative of religious animosity that lingered for generations.

The scars left by the destruction of temples cast shadows over subsequent interactions between Hindu and Muslim communities. The memory of these events, passed down through oral traditions and historical accounts, contributed to the shaping of collective identities and perceptions.

- **Rebuilding and Reconciliation**

In the wake of such historical traumas, the story of Hindu-Muslim relations also includes instances of rebuilding and reconciliation. Some rulers, recognizing the need for social cohesion, supported the reconstruction of temples and the restoration of religious harmony.

The Maratha ruler, Shivaji, for instance, emphasized religious tolerance and even started the reconstruction of temples that had been destroyed during previous invasions. This approach reflected a nuanced understanding of the diverse fabric of the Indian subcontinent, acknowledging the importance of coexistence amidst religious differences.

- **Modern Perspectives**

As we step into the present, the echoes of temple destruction reverberate in contemporary debates on cultural heritage, religious freedom, and historical preservation. Efforts to reclaim and restore temples that have been neglected or damaged over the centuries highlight the ongoing significance of these historical sites.

In recent times, there has been a growing awareness of the need to preserve India's cultural heritage, irrespective of religious affiliations. This shift in perspective aims to foster a shared sense of ownership over the nation's historical legacy, emphasizing the interconnectedness of Hindu and Muslim contributions to the cultural mosaic of India.

The destruction of Hindu temples stands as a poignant chapter in the complex narrative of Hindu-Muslim relations in India. It is a tale of political conquests, religious zealotry, and cultural resilience. As we navigate the historical contours of this narrative, it becomes clear that understanding the nuances of temple destruction is crucial for fostering a more inclusive and harmonious future.

"Bridging Divides" seeks not only to unravel the historical intricacies of temple destruction but also to explore how these events have shaped contemporary perceptions and interactions. By acknowledging the shared heritage of both communities and recognizing the significance of cultural preservation, this exploration forms a crucial foundation for the subsequent chapters, where we delve into the challenges and opportunities of Hindu-Muslim relations in contemporary India.

Chapter 2: Burning of Universities and Libraries

In the annals of history, the burning of universities and libraries stands as a stark testament to the vulnerability of knowledge in times of social and political upheaval. This chapter delves into the historical events where seats of learning, repositories of wisdom, and custodians of cultural heritage were engulfed in flames, shaping the contours of Hindu-Muslim relations in the Indian subcontinent.

- **The Sanctuaries of Knowledge**

Universities and libraries have traditionally been revered as sanctuaries of knowledge, where scholars from diverse backgrounds congregate to exchange ideas, debate philosophies, and contribute to the intellectual fabric of society. In the rich landscape of ancient India, institutions like Nalanda and Taxila emerged as beacons of enlightenment, drawing students and teachers from across the known world.

However, the tranquillity of these centres of learning was not immune to the tides of history. The burning of universities and libraries unfolded as a tragic chapter, marking the loss of invaluable manuscripts, scientific treatises, and literary treasures.

- **Nalanda: A Beacon in Flames**

The ruins of Nalanda, nestled in present-day Bihar, serve as poignant reminders of the destruction wrought upon these bastions of knowledge. The sacking of Nalanda in the 12th century by Khilji forces was a watershed moment that reverberated through the corridors of history. The once-thriving centre of Buddhist learning, with its nine-story library and thousands of scholars, fell victim to an invasion that left an indelible scar on India's intellectual heritage.

The burning of Nalanda was not just an assault on a physical structure but an erasure of centuries of accumulated knowledge. The flames that engulfed its revered halls silenced the voices of countless philosophers, mathematicians, and theologians who had contributed to the intellectual vibrancy of the region.

- **Taxila: Echoes of a Lost Legacy**

Similarly, the ancient city of Taxila, a cradle of learning in what is now Pakistan, faced the ravages of time and conflict. Conquered by various forces, including the Huns and later the Islamic armies, Taxila witnessed the decline of its once-thriving educational institutions. The burning of Taxila's libraries and academic centres underscored the fragility of intellectual legacies in the face of geopolitical turmoil.
The loss of these centres of learning had repercussions that extended beyond their immediate physical destruction. It disrupted the transmission of knowledge, hindered the progression of scientific inquiry, and, perhaps most significantly, deepened the fault lines between communities.

- **Theological Tensions and Intellectual Spaces**

The burning of universities and libraries was often intertwined with theological tensions that permeated the fabric of mediaeval India. The clashes between religious ideologies, particularly those between Hinduism and Islam, manifested in the desecration of these intellectual spaces. Theological differences, fueled by zealotry and a desire for dominance, led to the intentional destruction of the very institutions that epitomised the pursuit of knowledge.
While historical records provide insights into the motivations behind these acts, they also reveal a complex interplay of power, politics, and religion. The burning of universities became a symbolic manifestation of the struggle for dominance, where intellectual supremacy was as sought after as territorial control.

- **Rebuilding the Foundations**

As embers cooled and the echoes of destruction reverberated through the ages, there emerged attempts to rebuild the foundations of intellectual heritage. The subsequent centuries saw the establishment of new centres of learning, with patrons and scholars seeking to revive the spirit of inquiry that had once flourished in Nalanda, Taxila, and other lost bastions of knowledge.

Under the patronage of various rulers, including the Mughals, a revival of scholarship took place. The creation of libraries, the translation of classical texts, and the synthesis of diverse intellectual traditions marked an attempt to reconstruct what had been lost. Yet, the scars of the past lingered, influencing the interactions between Hindu and Muslim communities in the years to come.

- **Modern Perspectives on Education**

The burning of universities and libraries remains a poignant chapter in the historical narrative, with implications reaching into the present day. As we examine contemporary educational landscapes, there is a recognition of the pivotal role that education plays in fostering understanding and harmony.

The emphasis on education as a means of enlightenment and empowerment has led to initiatives aimed at preserving and promoting cultural and intellectual diversity. Efforts to build inclusive educational systems that draw from the collective heritage of Hindu and Muslim traditions reflect a growing awareness of the importance of shared knowledge in forging a cohesive society.

- **Cultural Preservation and Communal Harmony**

The preservation of cultural heritage, including manuscripts, ancient texts, and artefacts, has become a shared endeavour. Museums, libraries, and academic institutions now serve as custodians of diverse cultural legacies, emphasising the interconnectedness of India's religious and intellectual traditions.

In recent times, collaborative projects and initiatives between Hindu and Muslim communities to preserve and celebrate shared cultural heritage have emerged. These efforts aim not only to mend historical wounds but also to build bridges between communities through a shared appreciation for the richness of their intellectual traditions. The burning of universities and libraries stands as a haunting chapter in the history of Hindu-Muslim relations, leaving imprints on the collective consciousness of the subcontinent. This chapter serves as a lens through which we can explore the complexities of intellectual history, theological tensions, and the enduring quest for knowledge. "Bridging Divides" recognizes the significance of education as a catalyst for understanding and cooperation. As we move forward in this exploration of Hindu-Muslim relations in contemporary India, the scars of burnt libraries and the echoes of lost wisdom compel us to reflect on the shared responsibility of preserving and fostering the intellectual heritage that unites, rather than divides, the diverse communities of the nation.

Chapter 3: Disdain for Idol Worship and Polytheism

In the kaleidoscope of India's religious landscape, the dynamic interplay between Hinduism and Islam has been shaped not only by shared histories but also by stark theological differences. Central among these differences is the disdain for idol worship and polytheism within certain strands of Islamic belief. This chapter delves into the theological contrasts that have historically fueled tensions between these two rich traditions, exploring how differing perspectives on the divine have contributed to the complexity of Hindu-Muslim relations.

- **Theological Foundations**

At the heart of the divergence between Hinduism and Islam lies a fundamental contrast in their understanding of the divine. Hinduism, with its diverse pantheon of deities and the practice of idol worship, stands in stark contrast to the Islamic principle of monotheism, encapsulated in the profound declaration: "There is no god but Allah, and Muhammad is His messenger."

The Islamic aversion to idol worship is deeply rooted in the theological foundations of the faith. The belief in the absolute oneness of God, or Tawhid, underscores the rejection of any form of association or representation of the divine. This theological stance has historically given rise to a certain disdain for the polytheistic practices prevalent in Hinduism.

- **Iconoclasm in Islamic History**

Historically, the disdain for idol worship found expression in acts of iconoclasm, where images and idols were systematically destroyed. This phenomenon is not unique to India but has occurred in various parts of the Islamic world over the centuries.

The spread of Islam into regions with diverse religious traditions often led to tensions over the veneration of sacred images. The destruction of idols and religious symbols during conquests became a manifestation of religious fervour and a commitment to the exclusive worship of the one true God.

- **Cultural Synthesis and Strain**

The theological disparities between Hinduism and Islam have been both a source of cultural synthesis and strain. While the Indian subcontinent witnessed the coexistence of these two traditions for centuries, the theological distinctions occasionally erupted into periods of conflict.

The Delhi Sultanate and the Mughal Empire, for instance, navigated the challenge of ruling over a predominantly Hindu population while upholding Islamic principles. The architectural marvels of the Mughals, such as the Taj Mahal, exemplify the synthesis of Islamic and indigenous artistic traditions. Yet, the theological gap persisted, and instances of iconoclasm and temple desecration marred this coexistence.

- **Symbolism and Misunderstandings**

The disdain for idol worship often extended beyond theological differences to become symbolic of cultural and religious divides. The physical destruction of idols and temples served not only as acts of religious purification but also as symbols of asserting dominance and imposing a particular worldview.

Misunderstandings surrounding the role of idols in Hindu worship further exacerbated tensions. From an Islamic perspective, the worship of idols was seen as a departure from the purity of monotheistic devotion. However, Hindu idol worship is deeply symbolic, representing a means of connecting with the divine rather than an act of attributing divinity to the physical form.

- **Shared Spaces and Interactions**

Despite theological disparities, shared spaces and interactions between Hindus and Muslims have been significant throughout history. In certain periods, rulers and leaders adopted policies of religious tolerance, fostering an environment where diverse religious practices could coexist.

Akbar, the Mughal emperor, is often cited as an example of a ruler who sought to bridge theological gaps. His initiative, Din-i Ilahi, aimed to synthesise elements of various religious traditions, creating a harmonious space for dialogue and understanding. While this endeavour did not gain widespread acceptance, it reflected an attempt to foster mutual respect between different religious communities.

- **Contemporary Interfaith Dialogue**

In contemporary times, the disdain for idol worship and polytheism is a nuanced aspect of Hindu-Muslim relations. Interfaith dialogue initiatives seek to bridge understanding between adherents of both traditions, emphasising common values and shared aspirations. Scholars, theologians, and activists engage in discussions that delve into the theological nuances of idol worship and monotheism. These dialogues aim not at convergence but at creating spaces where differences can be acknowledged and respected, fostering a culture of mutual understanding.

- **Cultural Appreciation**

Within the broader context of Hindu-Muslim relations, there has been a growing appreciation for the cultural and religious diversity that defines India. Efforts to recognize the significance of religious symbols and practices without necessarily adopting them have become integral to fostering a more inclusive society.
Cultural festivals, shared spaces of worship, and collaborative artistic endeavors have become avenues for celebrating diversity while acknowledging theological disparities. The exploration of each other's religious traditions with an open mind has the potential to transform disdain into appreciation.

- **Embracing Diversity**

Understanding the disdain for idol worship and polytheism within the context of Hindu-Muslim relations requires a nuanced appreciation for the complexity of religious beliefs. It is an exploration of the theological fault lines that have at times been a source of tension but also an opportunity for mutual enrichment.
As we continue our journey through the intricate tapestry of Hindu-Muslim relations, this chapter provides a crucial foundation for the subsequent exploration of challenges and initiatives aimed at fostering greater harmony. In recognizing and respecting theological differences, we pave the way for a future where diversity becomes a source of

strength rather than division. The disdain for idol worship and polytheism becomes not a point of contention, but a call for mutual understanding and respect on the shared path towards coexistence.

Chapter 4: Taxes on Non-Muslims

In the historical narrative of Hindu-Muslim relations in India, the imposition of special taxes on non-Muslims has been a chapter fraught with economic disparity and social tension. This chapter explores the historical context, the rationale behind these discriminatory taxes, and the impact they had on the relationships between Hindus and Muslims.

- **Jizya and Dhimmi Status**

The imposition of taxes on non-Muslims, notably the jizya, emerged from Islamic jurisprudence during the mediaeval period. Jizya was a poll tax levied on non-Muslims living under Islamic rule, signifying their acceptance of the protection provided by the Muslim state. Non-Muslims who paid the jizya were granted dhimmi status, affording them certain rights and protections under Islamic law.
While the concept of jizya itself had roots in early Islamic traditions, its application in the Indian subcontinent varied depending on the rulers and the prevailing political climate.

- **Historical Instances**

The Delhi Sultanate and later the Mughal Empire implemented the jizya as a means of generating revenue and solidifying the distinction between Muslims and non-Muslims. However, historical records suggest that the application of jizya was not consistent across all periods or regions.
Some rulers exercised flexibility in its implementation, while others enforced it rigorously. The imposition of discriminatory taxes became a reflection not only of economic policy but also of the power dynamics

between ruling Muslims and subject non-Muslim populations.

- **Economic Disparities**

The levying of special taxes on non-Muslims contributed to economic disparities, creating a distinction between the fiscal burdens borne by different religious communities. Non-Muslims faced financial obligations that were absent for their Muslim counterparts, perpetuating a sense of inequality within society.

The economic burden of discriminatory taxation had far-reaching consequences, affecting the socio-economic mobility of non-Muslim communities. It not only strained relations between Hindus and Muslims but also created economic fault lines that persisted through generations.

- **Impact on Interfaith Relations**

The imposition of taxes on non-Muslims strained interfaith relations, as it institutionalised a form of discrimination based on religious identity. While some rulers sought to maintain social harmony by providing economic incentives and protection to non-Muslims, the inherent inequality embedded in these policies fueled resentment and contributed to a sense of religious division.

The economic disparities reinforced perceptions of second-class citizenship for non-Muslims, further deepening the fissures between communities. The jizya, intended as a source of revenue, became a symbol of the unequal treatment meted out to non-Muslims under Islamic rule.

- **Evolving Perspectives**

As the Indian subcontinent witnessed changing political landscapes, the application of discriminatory taxes on non-Muslims evolved. The arrival of colonial powers marked a shift in governance structures, and the imposition of such taxes diminished.

The decline of discriminatory taxation in the colonial era did not, however, immediately erase the socio-economic disparities or alter deeply ingrained perceptions. The legacy of historical inequalities continued to shape the dynamics between Hindus and Muslims even after the cessation of such taxes.

- **Contemporary Implications**

In contemporary times, the legacy of discriminatory taxation resonates in discussions around secularism, equality, and social justice. The historical imposition of taxes on non-Muslims is cited as an example of the challenges faced by religious minorities and marginalised communities in the past.

Efforts towards building a more inclusive society emphasize the need to address historical injustices and rectify economic disparities. While discriminatory taxes may no longer be in place, the echoes of their impact persist in the socio-economic fabric of the nation.

- **Toward Inclusivity**

Understanding the historical imposition of taxes on non-Muslims is crucial for navigating contemporary interfaith relations. Recognizing the complexities of this historical chapter allows for a more nuanced exploration of the challenges and opportunities in fostering a harmonious society.

As we proceed in our exploration of Hindu-Muslim relations in contemporary India, this chapter serves as a reminder of the intricate ways in which economic policies have shaped social dynamics. By acknowledging historical injustices and working towards economic inclusivity, we lay the groundwork for a future where equality is not just a principle but a lived reality for all communities, irrespective of religious affiliations.

Chapter 5: Religious Divides and the Creation of Pakistan

The partition of British India in 1947, leading to the creation of Pakistan, stands as one of the most defining moments in the history of Hindu-Muslim relations on the Indian subcontinent. This chapter delves into the historical context, the factors that contributed to the demand for a separate Muslim state, and the profound impact that the partition had on the religious landscape and communal dynamics.

- **Pre-Partition Landscape**

The prelude to the creation of Pakistan was shaped by a complex tapestry of historical, political, and socio-religious factors. The Indian National Congress, representing a diverse array of communities, sought independence from British rule within a united India. However, as the demand for self-governance gained momentum, religious identities became increasingly salient.

The All India Muslim League, under the leadership of Muhammad Ali Jinnah, articulated the demand for a separate Muslim state. Jinnah's vision of Pakistan as a homeland for Muslims was grounded in the belief that Muslims needed a distinct political entity to safeguard their religious, cultural, and socio-economic interests.

- **Lahore Resolution: A Turning Point**

The Lahore Resolution of 1940, also known as the Pakistan Resolution, marked a turning point in the quest for a separate Muslim state. The resolution, passed during the All India Muslim League session in Lahore, called for the creation of independent states for Muslims in regions where they were in a majority. This laid the foundation for the demand for Pakistan as a separate nation for Muslims.

The Lahore Resolution reflected the growing sentiment among

Muslims that their distinct identity and interests could only be safeguarded through the establishment of a state where Islamic principles could be the guiding force.

- **Religious and Cultural Identity**

The call for Pakistan was not solely about political autonomy; it was deeply rooted in the desire to preserve and promote Islamic values and cultural identity. The two-nation theory, propounded by Jinnah, posited that Hindus and Muslims were distinct nations with their own religious, cultural, and social practices.

The demand for Pakistan underscored the belief that Muslims required a separate political entity to protect their religious traditions, especially in the face of a majority Hindu population in a united India. The envisioned state of Pakistan was seen as a haven where Muslims could practise their faith freely, without fear of religious assimilation or cultural dilution.

- **Communal Tensions and Violence**

The demand for Pakistan exacerbated communal tensions on the eve of partition. As the realization of a divided India loomed, communities were gripped by fear and uncertainty. Mass migrations, communal violence, and bloodshed marked the tragic events of 1947.

The partition led to one of the largest and most tragic population exchanges in history, with millions of Hindus and Sikhs migrating to India, and Muslims to Pakistan. The communal violence that accompanied the process resulted in immense human suffering, loss of life, and the uprooting of communities.

- **Impact on Hindu-Muslim Relations**

The creation of Pakistan had a profound impact on Hindu-Muslim

relations, transforming the communal landscape of the subcontinent. The partition left scars on the collective psyche of both communities, shaping perceptions and attitudes for generations to come.
The communal violence and forced migrations left a deep sense of mistrust and animosity. The wounds of partition continue to influence interfaith dynamics, as memories of the traumatic events persist within the oral histories of families and communities on both sides of the border.

- **Quest for Harmony and Reconciliation**

In the aftermath of the partition, both India and Pakistan embarked on separate paths, each grappling with the challenges of nation-building and communal harmony. In India, efforts were made to establish a secular and inclusive democracy, emphasizing the coexistence of diverse religious communities within a single nation.
However, the legacy of partition cast a long shadow over Hindu-Muslim relations in both countries. Despite shared cultural heritage and a history of coexistence, the events of 1947 left an enduring impact, influencing political narratives, social dynamics, and perceptions of the "other."

- **Contemporary Perspectives**

In contemporary times, the creation of Pakistan remains a historical touchstone that shapes the discourse on Hindu-Muslim relations. The shared history of India and Pakistan, characterised by periods of tension, conflict, and occasional cooperation, reflects the complexities of navigating religious identities within the subcontinent.
The partition experience continues to be remembered in cultural narratives, literature, and public discourse. The pain and trauma associated with the events of 1947 serve as a reminder of the importance of fostering understanding, dialogue, and empathy in the

pursuit of lasting harmony.

- **Communal Narratives and National Identity**

The partition not only divided the geography but also contributed to the shaping of distinct communal narratives and national identities. In India, the commitment to a secular and inclusive vision of the nation coexists with the memories of partition, providing a framework for diversity and coexistence.
In Pakistan, the creation of an Islamic state has shaped the national identity, with Islam serving as a unifying force. The partition experience, while central to the historical narrative, is also a reminder of the challenges and opportunities inherent in managing religious diversity.

The creation of Pakistan, rooted in the desire to safeguard Muslim identity and establish an independent state, profoundly altered the landscape of Hindu-Muslim relations. The events surrounding partition left an indelible mark on the historical narrative, influencing the dynamics between the two communities in the decades that followed.
As we continue our exploration of Hindu-Muslim relations in contemporary India, the partition remains a poignant chapter. It prompts reflection on the complexities of religious identity, the impact of historical events on communal dynamics, and the ongoing quest for harmony and reconciliation. The experiences of 1947 serve as a potent reminder of the need for understanding, empathy, and dialogue in building a shared future that transcends the scars of the past.

Chapter 6: Role of Extremism and Political Support

In the intricate tapestry of Hindu-Muslim relations in contemporary India, the role of extremism and political support has been a shaping force, influencing public discourse, social dynamics, and the overall trajectory of communal relations. This chapter delves into the complex interplay of extremist ideologies, political motivations, and their impact on the relationship between Hindus and Muslims.

- **Extremism: Ideological Underpinnings**

Extremist ideologies, rooted in religious fervour or political radicalism, have periodically surfaced within both Hindu and Muslim communities in India. These ideologies often emphasize exclusivity, perpetuating a narrative of 'us versus them' and contributing to the polarization of religious identities.
For some, extremist ideologies become a means of expressing grievances, real or perceived, and seeking redress through radical measures. The amplification of extremist voices can deepen existing fault lines, exacerbate communal tensions, and pose challenges to the fabric of a pluralistic society.

- **Political Instrumentalization**

The intertwining of extremism with political agendas has been a recurrent theme in the narrative of Hindu-Muslim relations. Some political actors, driven by electoral considerations or ideological inclinations, have been known to instrumentalize religious sentiments to consolidate their support base.
Extremist groups may find resonance within certain political circles, leading to the legitimization of their ideologies. In turn, political support provides a platform for the dissemination of extremist narratives, often amplifying tensions between communities for short-term gains.

- **Rise of Right-Wing Nationalism**

The rise of right-wing nationalism in recent decades has further complicated the dynamics of Hindu-Muslim relations. Some political entities espousing nationalist agendas have sought to assert a particular cultural and religious identity, often emphasizing the interests of the majority community.

While such movements may resonate with certain sections of the population, they can also contribute to an atmosphere of religious exclusivity, marginalizing minority communities. The alignment of extremist elements with right-wing nationalist movements has the potential to exacerbate communal tensions and challenge the principles of a secular democracy.

- **Islamist Extremism**

On the other side of the spectrum, Islamist extremist ideologies have also found a foothold in certain segments of the Muslim community. Movements advocating for the establishment of Sharia law or challenging perceived injustices against Muslims can, at times, adopt radical approaches.

The influence of global jihadist movements has added an international dimension to Islamist extremism in India. The radicalization of individuals, often facilitated by online platforms, poses security challenges and contributes to the complexity of addressing extremism within the Muslim community.

- **Political Support for Muslim Extremist**

While extremist ideologies and political support can contribute to communal tensions, it is essential to acknowledge efforts by political actors and movements that advocate for minority rights and social justice. There are instances where political leaders, irrespective of their religious affiliations, have championed the cause of inclusive governance and the protection of minority communities.

The articulation of policies that promote religious harmony, equal opportunities, and protection against discrimination contributes to a more inclusive vision of the nation. Political entities that prioritise pluralism and diversity play a crucial role in counteracting the influence of extremism and fostering positive interfaith relations.

- **Secularism and Constitutional Safeguards**

India's secular ethos, enshrined in its constitution, serves as a foundational principle for governance. The state is mandated to treat all citizens equally, irrespective of their religious affiliations. Constitutional safeguards aim to protect minority rights, ensuring that individuals are free to practise their faith without fear of discrimination.

Political leaders who uphold the secular fabric of the nation contribute to an environment that discourages the instrumentalization of religion for political gains. However, the implementation of these principles faces challenges, and the delicate balance between secularism and religious identity remains an ongoing societal conversation.

- **Countering Extremism: Role of Civil Society**

Civil society, including non-governmental organisations, religious leaders, and grassroots movements, plays a crucial role in countering extremism and promoting interfaith understanding. Initiatives focused on dialogue, community engagement, and education contribute to building bridges between Hindus and Muslims.

Promoting civic values, tolerance, and respect for diversity is essential in combating the divisive impact of extremist ideologies. Civil society efforts complement constitutional safeguards, providing avenues for individuals from different communities to come together, understand each other's perspectives, and work towards common goals.

The role of extremism and political support is a multifaceted aspect of Hindu-Muslim relations in contemporary India. The interplay of

radical ideologies and political motivations can either deepen existing divisions or contribute to the forging of a more inclusive society.
As we navigate the complexities of this relationship, it is crucial to recognize the diversity within each religious community and the potential for shared values and aspirations. Efforts towards countering extremism, promoting secularism, and fostering positive interfaith relations are vital for building a harmonious society that respects the rights and identities of all its citizens. The challenges are significant, but the collective commitment to pluralism, tolerance, and understanding can pave the way for a more united and inclusive India.

Chapter 7: Sharia and the Legal System

In the multifaceted landscape of Hindu-Muslim relations in India, the role of Sharia, the Islamic legal system, has been a subject of both legal and cultural significance. This chapter explores the coexistence of Sharia alongside the broader legal framework in India, shedding light on the complexities and intersections between religious law and the secular legal system.

- **Coexistence of Legal Systems**

India, as a secular and diverse nation, accommodates various personal laws for different religious communities. The coexistence of these legal systems, Many Political parties support Sharia for Muslims to get Muslims votes, They support muslim laws on matters such as marriage, divorce, inheritance, and family relations among Muslims. However Current government supports UCC.
While personal laws provide communities the autonomy to regulate their internal affairs based on religious principles, they operate within the overarching framework of the Indian legal system. The Constitution of India, as the supreme law of the land, guarantees fundamental rights to all citizens, ensuring that personal laws do not infringe upon these rights.

- **Sharia and Family Law**

Sharia holds particular significance in matters of family law for Muslims. The Muslim Personal Law (Shariat) Application Act of 1937 formalised the application of Islamic law in India, providing a legal framework for matters such as marriage, divorce, maintenance, and succession within the Muslim community.

The application of Sharia in family law matters allows Muslims to follow their religious principles in these aspects of life. However, this coexistence of personal and secular legal systems has at times led to debates and discussions about the need for reforms within personal laws to align them with contemporary notions of justice and equality.

- **Debates and Reforms**

The coexistence of Sharia within the legal system has been a subject of ongoing debates and discussions. Some argue for reforms within personal laws to address perceived gender inequalities and align them with modern notions of justice. Calls for reforms within the Muslim personal law system have led to discussions on issues such as triple talaq (divorce) and the age of marriage for Muslim women.

While debates around personal laws, including Sharia, reflect the evolving socio-cultural landscape, any proposed reforms must navigate a delicate balance between respecting religious autonomy and ensuring the protection of fundamental rights for all citizens.

- **Constitutional Safeguards**

The Indian Constitution provides safeguards to protect the rights of individuals, including those from religious minorities. Article 25 guarantees the right to freedom of religion, allowing every citizen the right to freely profess, practice, and propagate their religion. This includes the right to follow personal laws based on religious beliefs. However, the exercise of these rights is subject to reasonable restrictions to ensure public order, morality, and the well-being of individuals. The constitutional framework serves as a guiding principle, ensuring that personal laws, including Sharia, operate within the broader contours of justice, equality, and individual rights.

- **Parallel Legal Systems**

The coexistence of Sharia and the secular legal system raises questions about the challenges posed by parallel legal systems within a diverse society. While personal laws provide communities the freedom to regulate their internal affairs, they must align with constitutional principles and protect the fundamental rights of individuals.
Efforts towards legal reforms, when deemed necessary, must navigate sensitivities surrounding religious autonomy while addressing concerns related to justice and equality. Striking this balance is crucial for fostering a legal framework that respects cultural diversity while upholding the principles of a secular and inclusive society.

- **Harmony and Challenges**

The coexistence of Sharia and the legal system reflects the harmony and challenges inherent in India's diverse social fabric. On one hand, personal laws allow communities to maintain their distinct religious identity and traditions. On the other hand, the need for periodic reviews and reforms arises to address evolving social norms and ensure the protection of individual rights.
The challenges lie in navigating these complexities with sensitivity and inclusivity. Legal reforms, when undertaken, should involve inclusive consultations with stakeholders from the respective communities to foster a sense of ownership and understanding.

Muslim personal law within the legal system of a secular and diverse nation like India reflects the country's commitment to upholding religious freedom and accommodating cultural diversity. The interplay between personal and secular legal systems poses challenges but also provides an opportunity for dialogue, understanding, and reforms that align with the principles of justice, equality, and individual rights.

Chapter 8: Government Initiatives: Jobs, Infrastructure, Business Opportunities, and Healthcare

In the complex tapestry of Hindu-Muslim relations in contemporary India, the role of government initiatives in providing opportunities and addressing socio-economic disparities is pivotal. This chapter explores various initiatives undertaken by the government to promote inclusivity, create economic opportunities, and improve healthcare infrastructure for all citizens, irrespective of religious affiliations.

- **Employment Opportunities**

One of the critical aspects of fostering inclusivity is ensuring equal access to employment opportunities. Government initiatives aimed at job creation and skill development play a significant role in empowering communities economically.

Programs such as Skill India and Make in India focus on enhancing the skill set of individuals and promoting entrepreneurship. By providing training in various industries, these initiatives aim to bridge the gap between demand and supply in the job market, fostering economic growth and reducing unemployment rates.

- **Reservation Policies**

The Indian government has implemented reservation policies to address historical socio-economic imbalances. Affirmative action measures, including reservations in education and public sector

employment, aim to uplift marginalised communities, including religious minorities.
Reservation policies, while a subject of debate, have been instrumental in providing opportunities for individuals from economically and socially disadvantaged backgrounds. These policies contribute to a more inclusive workforce and help in dismantling barriers that hinder equitable access to resources.

- **Infrastructure Development**

Infrastructure development is a cornerstone of economic progress and social well-being. Government initiatives focused on building robust infrastructure, including roads, transportation, and connectivity, contribute to overall development and bridge regional disparities. Projects like the Pradhan Mantri Gram Sadak Yojana (PMGSY) aim to connect rural areas with urban centres, providing accessibility and opening avenues for economic activities. Such initiatives play a crucial role in ensuring that the benefits of development reach all corners of the country, fostering a sense of inclusivity.

- **Business Opportunities and Financial Inclusion**

Promoting entrepreneurship and ensuring financial inclusion are key components of government initiatives to empower citizens economically. Schemes like Stand-Up India, aimed at supporting businesses run by women and individuals from Scheduled Castes and Scheduled Tribes, contribute to a more inclusive economic landscape. Financial inclusion initiatives, including the Jan Dhan Yojana, focus on bringing marginalized communities into the formal banking sector. This not only facilitates access to credit but also encourages savings and investment, empowering individuals to participate more actively in economic activities.

- **Healthcare Initiatives**

Access to healthcare is a fundamental right, and government initiatives in the healthcare sector are essential for fostering the well-being of citizens. Programs like Ayushman Bharat, the world's largest government-funded healthcare program, aim to provide financial protection against catastrophic health expenditures.Through Ayushman Bharat, millions of families, including those from economically disadvantaged backgrounds, have gained access to quality healthcare services. The program underscores the government's commitment to ensuring that health services are accessible and affordable for all citizens.

- **Minority Welfare Schemes**

Specific schemes targeted at the welfare of minority communities, including Muslims, recognize the unique challenges they may face. Initiatives like the Multi-Sectoral Development Program (MsDP) aim to address the development deficits in identified minority concentration areas, focusing on education, healthcare, and skill development.

These targeted schemes acknowledge the need for nuanced interventions to address the socio-economic disparities that may exist within minority communities. By tailoring programs to specific needs, the government seeks to ensure that the benefits of development reach every section of society.

- **Challenges and Opportunities**

While government initiatives play a crucial role in fostering inclusivity, challenges persist. Ensuring the effective implementation of policies, addressing regional disparities, and overcoming socio-cultural barriers require sustained efforts.

Ensuring that the benefits of development reach the most marginalized sections of society, including religious minorities, is an ongoing challenge. Initiatives need to be adaptive, responsive to changing socio-economic landscapes, and informed by feedback from the communities they aim to serve.

- **Role of Civil Society and Collaboration**

Government initiatives are more effective when complemented by the efforts of civil society organisations and community engagement. Collaborative efforts between the government, non-governmental organisations (NGOs), and local communities contribute to a more holistic approach to development.

Civil society can play a crucial role in ensuring that government initiatives are inclusive, transparent, and responsive to the needs of diverse communities. By fostering partnerships and encouraging participatory development, the impact of initiatives can be maximised.

- **Future Directions and Aspirations**

As India progresses on its path of development, the role of government initiatives in promoting inclusivity becomes increasingly critical. Future directions should involve a continued focus on addressing socio-economic disparities, improving access to education and healthcare, and creating an environment that encourages entrepreneurship and innovation.

The aspirations for an inclusive society require a collective commitment from all stakeholders – government, civil society, and citizens. By fostering an environment that values diversity and prioritises the well-being of every individual, India can continue its journey towards becoming a more equitable and inclusive nation.

Government initiatives in the realms of employment, infrastructure, business opportunities, and healthcare are integral to shaping the socio-economic landscape of contemporary India. These initiatives, when designed and implemented effectively, contribute to fostering inclusivity, breaking down barriers, and ensuring that the benefits of development reach all citizens.

Chapter 9: Uniting India through Uniform Civil Code

The idea of a Uniform Civil Code (UCC) has been a subject of extensive discourse in the context of Hindu-Muslim relations in India. This chapter explores the concept of a UCC, its historical background, the debates surrounding its implementation, and the potential role it could play in fostering unity and social cohesion in the diverse fabric of the nation.

- **Historical Context**

The call for a Uniform Civil Code traces its roots to the debates during the drafting of the Indian Constitution. The framers of the Constitution envisioned a uniform set of laws that would replace the existing personal laws based on religious practices. However, due to the sensitive nature of the issue and the diversity of religious communities in India, the framers chose to leave the decision to implement a UCC to future lawmakers.

- **What is a Uniform Civil Code?**

A Uniform Civil Code is essentially a single set of secular laws governing personal matters such as marriage, divorce, inheritance, and adoption for all citizens, irrespective of their religious affiliations. The objective is to promote gender justice, equality, and a sense of national unity by establishing a common legal framework for personal matters.

- **Gender Justice and Equality**

One of the key arguments in favour of a UCC is the promotion of gender justice and equality. India's existing personal laws, including those based on religious practices, often have provisions that can be perceived as discriminatory towards women. A UCC, proponents argue, could rectify these disparities and provide equal rights and protection to all citizens, regardless of their religious background.

- **Fostering National Unity**

A UCC is seen by many as a step towards fostering national unity by transcending religious divides. The existence of distinct personal laws based on religious affiliations is often viewed as a source of division, reinforcing the idea of separate communities. A common civil code, it is argued, would contribute to a sense of oneness and unity among the diverse population of India.

- **Debates and Opposition**

Despite its potential benefits, the idea of a UCC has faced significant opposition and debates. Critics argue that imposing a uniform code could infringe upon the cultural and religious autonomy of communities. There are concerns that a UCC might be perceived as an attempt to homogenise diverse religious practices, leading to resistance from religious and cultural groups.
Some fear that implementing a UCC without due consideration for the sensitivities of different communities could lead to social unrest. The historical context of religious diversity in India necessitates careful consideration and consensus-building to ensure that any move towards a UCC is inclusive and respects the plurality of the nation.

- **Implementation Challenges**

The practical challenges of implementing a Uniform Civil Code are

complex. India's social fabric is woven with diverse religious and cultural traditions, each with its unique set of beliefs and practices. The process of arriving at a consensus that respects this diversity while establishing common ground is daunting.
There are concerns about the potential resistance from conservative factions within various communities. Achieving consensus on issues related to personal laws, which are deeply intertwined with religious beliefs, requires a delicate balance between principles of justice, individual rights, and respect for cultural identities.

- **International Comparisons**

The discourse on a Uniform Civil Code often draws comparisons with other countries that have adopted such codes. Countries like France and Turkey have implemented uniform civil codes to varying degrees. However, the contextual differences in terms of historical, cultural, and religious diversity highlight the need for a nuanced and India-specific approach.
Understanding the experiences of other nations can offer insights into the challenges and benefits of implementing a UCC. It underscores the importance of context-specific solutions that consider the unique socio-cultural dynamics of each country.

- **Inclusive Approach and Dialogue**

Any move towards a Uniform Civil Code must adopt an inclusive approach that involves active dialogue with various religious and cultural communities. Sensitivity to the diverse perspectives and a commitment to preserving cultural identities are paramount in the formulation of any common civil code.
Inclusivity should extend beyond political and legal circles to include representatives from civil society, religious leaders, and community members. A collaborative approach ensures that the concerns and

aspirations of all stakeholders are taken into account, fostering a sense of ownership and understanding.

- **Steps Towards Reform**

Rather than imposing a sudden and sweeping change, a gradual and phased approach towards legal reforms could be considered. Addressing specific issues within personal laws that are perceived as discriminatory or outdated might serve as a pragmatic starting point. This could involve a series of targeted reforms that align with the principles of justice and equality.

Reform initiatives should be accompanied by robust awareness campaigns to educate the public about the intended changes and dispel misconceptions. Public participation and discourse are crucial elements in building consensus and garnering support for reforms related to personal laws.

The idea of a Uniform Civil Code represents a complex and multifaceted issue at the intersection of law, religion, and cultural diversity in India. While proponents argue that a UCC could contribute to gender justice, equality, and national unity, the opposition highlights concerns about preserving cultural autonomy and potential resistance from religious communities.

Navigating the path towards a Uniform Civil Code requires a delicate balance between the principles of justice, individual rights, and the preservation of cultural identities. Inclusive dialogue, involving representatives from various communities and civil society, is crucial for building consensus and ensuring that any reforms are contextual and respectful of India's rich diversity.

Chapter 10: Applying the Singapore Technique for Religious Harmony

Religious harmony is a delicate balance that many diverse nations strive to achieve, and Singapore has often been lauded for successfully navigating the complexities of coexistence among its various religious communities. This chapter explores the "Singapore Technique" for religious harmony, examining the policies, practices, and principles that contribute to fostering unity and understanding among different religious groups in the city-state.

- **Historical Context**

Singapore, with its multicultural and multi-religious population, has a unique historical background that shaped its approach to religious harmony. The city-state gained independence in 1965, and its leaders recognized early on the potential challenges posed by religious and ethnic diversity. The need for a cohesive and harmonious society became a cornerstone of Singapore's nation-building efforts.

- **Legal Framework**

One of the key elements of the Singapore Technique is a robust legal framework that safeguards religious freedoms while preventing religious tensions. The Maintenance of Religious Harmony Act (MRHA), enacted in 1990, empowers the government to take preventive measures against individuals or groups that incite religious hatred or discord.
The MRHA underscores Singapore's commitment to maintaining a secular state while respecting the rights of individuals to practise their religions freely. This legal framework serves as a deterrent against religious extremism and promotes a climate of respect and tolerance.

- **Inter-Religious Confidence Circles**

To facilitate dialogue and understanding among different religious communities, Singapore established Inter-Religious Confidence Circles (IRCCs). These circles bring together leaders and representatives from various religions to engage in open and constructive conversations. The

goal is to build trust, promote mutual respect, and address potential sources of tension before they escalate.
IRCCs are active at both the national and local levels, fostering relationships among religious leaders and their congregations. Through these initiatives, Singapore encourages continuous communication and collaboration, contributing to a sense of shared responsibility for religious harmony.

- **Education and Interfaith Understanding**

Singapore places a strong emphasis on education as a tool for promoting interfaith understanding. Religious and moral education is incorporated into the national curriculum, fostering an appreciation for different faiths from an early age. This approach aims to nurture a generation that values diversity and respects various religious beliefs. Interfaith dialogues and educational programs are conducted regularly to deepen understanding and dispel misconceptions. By fostering an environment of inclusivity within educational institutions, Singapore seeks to mould a society where individuals can coexist harmoniously, irrespective of their religious backgrounds.

- **Celebrating Religious Diversity**

Singapore actively promotes the celebration of religious diversity through various means. Public holidays are designated for major festivals of different religions, allowing citizens to participate in and appreciate the cultural and religious practices of their fellow residents. This recognition of diverse celebrations contributes to a sense of belonging for all communities.
The government supports and funds cultural events and religious celebrations, emphasising the importance of mutual respect and understanding. These initiatives not only showcase the richness of Singapore's religious tapestry but also provide opportunities for

different communities to come together in celebration.

- **Zero Tolerance for Hate Speech**

Singapore adopts a zero-tolerance approach towards hate speech and any form of religious discrimination. Strict laws are in place to penalise individuals or groups that engage in activities that could incite religious discord. This proactive stance aims to prevent the escalation of tensions and maintain a harmonious social fabric.

By swiftly addressing instances of hate speech or discrimination, Singapore sends a clear message that such behaviour will not be tolerated. This approach serves as a deterrent, discouraging actions that could undermine the city-state's commitment to religious harmony.

- **Social Integration Policies**

Beyond legal measures, Singapore implements social integration policies to foster interaction among different religious and ethnic communities. Public housing is intentionally designed to be ethnically and religiously diverse, encouraging residents from various backgrounds to live side by side.

Through initiatives like the Housing and Development Board's Ethnic Integration Policy, Singapore promotes mixed communities, preventing the formation of ethnic or religious enclaves. This intentional blending contributes to social cohesion and facilitates the organic development of friendships and understanding among diverse residents.

- **Challenges and Ongoing Efforts**

While Singapore's approach to religious harmony has been widely praised, it is not without its challenges. The city-state acknowledges the need for ongoing efforts to address emerging issues, especially in the context of global trends such as the rise of extremism and online radicalization.

Singapore continues to refine and adapt its strategies, incorporating new technologies and educational tools to promote interfaith understanding. The city-state recognizes that maintaining religious harmony is a continuous process that requires vigilance, adaptability, and the active involvement of all segments of society.

- **Lessons for Global Consideration**

The Singapore Technique for religious harmony offers valuable lessons for nations grappling with the complexities of diversity. The city-state's commitment to a secular state, a robust legal framework, and proactive measures to foster interfaith understanding provide a blueprint that can be adapted to various contexts.

Key takeaways include the importance of inclusive legal frameworks, the proactive engagement of religious leaders, and the intentional promotion of interfaith dialogue and understanding. Singapore's success in managing religious diversity demonstrates the potential for harmonious coexistence when these elements are thoughtfully integrated into national policies.

The Singapore Technique for religious harmony stands as a testament to the city-state's commitment to building a cohesive, multicultural society. By combining legal measures, social integration policies, and educational initiatives, Singapore has successfully navigated the complexities of religious diversity.

As nations around the world grapple with the challenges of fostering unity amidst diversity, the Singaporean experience offers valuable insights. The intentional promotion of interfaith understanding, the celebration of religious diversity, and a commitment to zero tolerance for hate speech provide a framework that can inspire and inform efforts toward religious harmony on a global scale.

In adopting and adapting the principles of the Singapore Technique, nations can aspire to build societies where individuals of different religious backgrounds coexist peacefully, respecting each other's beliefs and contributing to a shared vision of a harmonious and inclusive future.

Chapter 11: Initiatives by the Modi Government

The tenure of Prime Minister Narendra Modi has been marked by a slew of initiatives aimed at addressing various challenges facing India, including those related to religious and social harmony. This chapter explores key initiatives undertaken by the Modi government to promote inclusivity, economic development, and social cohesion, while also acknowledging the diversity and complexity of India's socio-political landscape.

- **Sabka Saath, Sabka Vikas**

The motto "Sabka Saath, Sabka Vikas" (Collective Effort, Inclusive Growth) encapsulates the overarching philosophy of the Modi government. The idea is to ensure the development and well-being of all sections of society, transcending religious, caste, and regional boundaries. Through this approach, the government seeks to create an environment where every citizen can actively participate in the nation's progress.

- **Jan Dhan Yojana**

Launched in 2014, the Pradhan Mantri Jan Dhan Yojana (PMJDY) aimed to promote financial inclusion by providing banking services to all citizens. The initiative focused on opening bank accounts for those who were previously unbanked, especially in rural areas. By fostering economic inclusion, the Jan Dhan Yojana sought to empower individuals and households, irrespective of their socio-religious backgrounds.

- **Swachh Bharat Abhiyan**

The Swachh Bharat Abhiyan, or Clean India Mission, was launched in 2014 with the goal of achieving a clean and open-defecation-free India. The initiative emphasized the importance of sanitation and hygiene, addressing challenges that disproportionately affected marginalised communities. By promoting cleanliness and access to sanitation facilities, the government aimed to improve the overall well-being of citizens, irrespective of their religious affiliations.

- **Beti Bachao, Beti Padhao**

The Beti Bachao, Beti Padhao (Save the Girl Child, Educate the Girl Child) initiative was launched to address the issue of declining child sex ratios and promote the education and well-being of girls. The campaign focused on challenging societal attitudes towards the girl child and encouraging families to invest in their daughters' education. This initiative aimed to empower girls and women across religious and socio-economic spectra.

- **Skill India**

Recognizing the importance of skill development in fostering economic opportunities, the Skill India initiative was launched to provide training and employment to the youth. The program aimed to equip individuals with the skills needed for various industries, thus contributing to reducing unemployment rates and promoting inclusive economic growth.

- **Ayushman Bharat**

Launched in 2018, Ayushman Bharat is considered one of the world's largest government-funded healthcare programs. The initiative aims to provide financial protection against catastrophic health expenditures by offering health insurance coverage to vulnerable and economically disadvantaged sections of society. Ayushman Bharat underscores the government's commitment to ensuring access to quality healthcare for all citizens, irrespective of their religious backgrounds.

- **Ujjwala Yojana**

The Pradhan Mantri Ujjwala Yojana, launched in 2016, focuses on providing free LPG (liquefied petroleum gas) connections to below-poverty-line households. By promoting clean cooking fuel, the initiative aims to improve the health and well-being of women, particularly in rural areas. This targeted approach contributes to uplifting vulnerable communities, irrespective of their religious affiliations.

- **Triple Talaq Legislation**

In a significant legislative move, the Modi government enacted the Muslim Women (Protection of Rights on Marriage) Act in 2019, criminalising the practice of instant triple talaq. The legislation aimed to empower Muslim women by safeguarding their rights and protecting them from the arbitrary and instantaneous dissolution of marriage. While the move was hailed by many as a step towards gender justice, it also sparked debates around the need for legal reforms within personal laws.

- **Atmanirbhar Bharat Abhiyan**

Launched in response to the economic challenges posed by the COVID-19 pandemic, the Atmanirbhar Bharat Abhiyan (Self-Reliant India Mission) seeks to stimulate economic growth, create employment, and enhance self-reliance across sectors. The initiative includes a range of measures to support businesses, promote innovation, and bolster economic resilience. The overarching goal is to create a self-reliant and globally competitive India that benefits citizens from all walks of life.

- **Education Initiatives**

The government has rolled out several education initiatives to enhance access to quality education. The Pradhan Mantri Scholarship Yojana for students from minority communities, the National Education Policy 2020, and efforts to promote digital literacy are among the various measures aimed at fostering educational inclusivity. These initiatives contribute to empowering individuals, irrespective of their religious backgrounds, through access to knowledge and skill development.

- **Addressing Extremism and Illegal Immigration**

The Modi government has taken a firm stance against extremism and illegal immigration. Policies such as the National Register of Citizens (NRC) and the Citizenship Amendment Act (CAA) have been implemented with the aim of addressing issues related to citizenship and immigration. These policies, while contentious and subject to diverse opinions, are framed within the broader context of national security and governance.

- **Pradhan Mantri Awas Yojana**

Launched in 2015, the Pradhan Mantri Awas Yojana (PMAY) aims to provide affordable housing to all citizens, with a particular focus on the economically weaker sections of society. The initiative recognizes the importance of secure housing in enhancing the overall quality of life for individuals and families, irrespective of their religious affiliations.

- **Digital India**

The Digital India initiative seeks to transform India into a digitally empowered society and knowledge economy. Through measures such as the widespread adoption of digital technologies, the promotion of e-governance, and the expansion of digital literacy, the government aims to bridge the digital divide and create equal opportunities for citizens across regions and communities.

- **Challenges and Criticisms**

While these initiatives demonstrate the government's commitment to inclusive development, they are not without challenges and criticisms. Some policies have sparked debates on issues such as religious freedom, economic disparities, and social justice. Critics argue that certain measures may disproportionately impact marginalised communities and call for a more nuanced and consultative approach in policy making.

The initiatives undertaken by the Modi government reflect a multifaceted approach to addressing the diverse challenges facing India. From economic development and healthcare to education and social reforms, these initiatives aim to create an inclusive and self-reliant nation. While each policy has its own set of critiques and debates, the overarching goal remains focused on holistic development that benefits all citizens, irrespective of their religious or socio-economic backgrounds.

As India navigates its path towards progress, the success of these initiatives will depend on their effective implementation, continuous refinement, and a commitment to addressing the evolving needs of the diverse population. In shaping the socio-political landscape, the initiatives of the Modi government contribute to the ongoing narrative of a nation striving for inclusive growth and prosperity.

Chapter 12: Tackling Extremism and Immigration

Addressing extremism and managing immigration are complex challenges that many nations grapple with in the contemporary world. In the Indian context, these issues have been subjects of intense debate and policy making. This chapter explores the measures taken by the Indian government to tackle extremism and manage immigration, examining the motivations behind these policies, their implications, and the broader socio-political context.

- **Extremism in India**

India, with its rich tapestry of cultures and religions, has had to confront challenges related to extremism. Various forms of extremism, ranging from religious fundamentalism to separatist movements, have posed threats to the nation's security and social harmony. The government's response to these challenges has been shaped by a commitment to maintaining law and order, safeguarding national security, and promoting communal harmony.

- **National Register of Citizens (NRC)**

The National Register of Citizens (NRC) is a government initiative aimed at creating a comprehensive list of genuine Indian citizens. The pilot project was implemented in the state of Assam to identify and exclude illegal immigrants, primarily those who entered the country after the Bangladesh Liberation War in 1971. The NRC process involves scrutinising documents to verify citizenship status, and those failing to provide adequate documentation may be deemed non-citizens.

The NRC has been a subject of controversy, with debates around its effectiveness, potential exclusion errors, and concerns about its impact on marginalised communities. Critics argue that the implementation of the NRC may lead to the exclusion of genuine citizens, particularly those from economically disadvantaged backgrounds.

- **Citizenship Amendment Act (CAA)**

The Citizenship Amendment Act (CAA), passed in 2019, provides a pathway to Indian citizenship for religious minorities from neighbouring countries, including Hindus, Sikhs, Christians, Buddhists, Jains, and Parsis, who faced persecution in those countries. The CAA is often discussed in conjunction with the NRC, with the government asserting that the CAA aims to protect persecuted minorities, while critics express concerns about potential discrimination and the exclusion of certain religious groups.
The CAA and NRC have been the focus of widespread protests and debates, with discussions ranging from questions about religious discrimination to concerns about the impact on India's secular fabric. The government has emphasised that these measures are aimed at addressing historical injustices and protecting vulnerable communities.

- **Counterterrorism Measures**

Tackling extremism involves comprehensive counterterrorism measures to ensure the security of the nation and its citizens. India has faced numerous terrorist attacks, and the government has undertaken initiatives to enhance intelligence gathering, strengthen security forces, and collaborate with international partners to combat terrorism. Counterterrorism efforts also involve addressing the root causes of extremism, including socio-economic disparities, lack of education, and ideological indoctrination. Initiatives such as community engagement, de-radicalization programs, and intelligence-sharing mechanisms are integral to the government's strategy to counter extremism.

- **Challenges and Criticisms**

While the government's efforts to tackle extremism and manage immigration are framed within the broader context of national security and governance, these measures have faced criticism and challenges. Critics argue that certain policies may disproportionately affect marginalised communities, raise questions about religious freedom, and potentially undermine the principles of inclusivity and diversity enshrined in the Indian Constitution.

The NRC and CAA, in particular, have sparked concerns about their impact on religious minorities and marginalised groups, leading to protests and debates both within India and on the international stage. The complex socio-political landscape of India requires nuanced policymaking that addresses the legitimate security concerns while safeguarding the rights and dignity of all citizens.

- **The Importance of Inclusive Dialogue**

Navigating the challenges posed by extremism and immigration requires an inclusive approach that involves dialogue, consultation, and a commitment to upholding constitutional values. Inclusive dialogue allows for a better understanding of the concerns and aspirations of different communities, fostering a sense of national unity and shared responsibility.

Engaging with civil society organisations, religious leaders, and community representatives is crucial to building consensus and ensuring that policies are framed with sensitivity to diverse perspectives. A collaborative approach that acknowledges the complexities of the issues at hand can contribute to more effective and inclusive solutions.

- **Balancing Security and Inclusivity**

Finding the right balance between ensuring national security and upholding inclusivity is a delicate task. Policymakers must navigate a complex terrain that considers the security imperatives while safeguarding individual rights and promoting social harmony. Striking this balance involves crafting policies that address the root causes of extremism, provide avenues for inclusive development, and protect the rights of all citizens.

- **International Collaboration**

Given the global nature of extremism and migration challenges, international collaboration is essential. India actively participates in regional and global forums to share intelligence, collaborate on counterterrorism efforts, and engage in discussions about managing migration. A coordinated approach that involves cooperation with neighbouring countries and the international community enhances the effectiveness of measures aimed at tackling extremism and managing immigration.

Tackling extremism and managing immigration are multifaceted challenges that require careful consideration, inclusive policy making, and a commitment to upholding democratic values. The initiatives undertaken by the Indian government reflect an effort to address security concerns while navigating the complexities of the nation's diversity.

As India continues to grapple with these challenges, it is essential to foster inclusive dialogue, engage with diverse perspectives, and ensure that policies are framed with sensitivity and respect for the rights of all citizens. Striking the right balance between security imperatives and inclusivity remains a dynamic and ongoing process, and the success of these initiatives will depend on their adaptability, effectiveness, and alignment with the principles of a diverse and pluralistic nation.

Summery

In the intricate exploration of Hindu-Muslim relations in India, spanning historical grievances, contemporary challenges, and governmental initiatives, a comprehensive narrative emerges. This journey through the chapters weaves a story that transcends temporal boundaries, reflecting the complexities and nuances of a relationship shaped by diverse historical, socio-political, and cultural threads.

The initial chapters delved into the historical wounds of the destruction of Hindu temples, the burning of universities, and the disdain for idol worship. These chapters provided a context for understanding the depth of historical tensions that have, at times, strained the fabric of Hindu-Muslim relations. Yet, in this historical exploration, glimpses of cultural exchange, coexistence, and shared heritage emerged, underscoring the resilience of the Indian subcontinent to assimilate diverse influences.

The examination of taxes on non-Muslims, the creation of Pakistan, and the role of extremism and political support illustrated the impact of political decisions on the social dynamics between Hindus and Muslims. The partition of India, a pivotal moment in history, left lasting imprints on the collective consciousness of both communities. The chapters underscored the challenges posed by extremism, with political support shaping the course of events. Amidst these challenges, the narrative revealed the enduring spirit of communities striving to coexist and navigate the complexities of a diverse society.

Transitioning to government initiatives, the exploration detailed a multifaceted approach by the Modi government. Initiatives such as Ayushman Bharat, Skill India, and the push for a Uniform Civil Code reflected a commitment to inclusive development. These policies aimed to bridge socio-economic gaps, provide healthcare, and promote education, emphasizing the government's role in fostering unity and equitable progress.

The analysis of the Singapore Technique for Religious Harmony added an international perspective, showcasing the importance of legal frameworks, interfaith dialogue, and inclusive policies. Singapore's model offered insights into how nations could manage religious diversity by emphasizing shared values and mutual understanding. The international lens contributed a broader perspective to the nuanced dynamics of Hindu-Muslim relations.

The subsequent exploration of measures tackling extremism and immigration presented a delicate balancing act. The National Register of Citizens (NRC) and the Citizenship Amendment Act (CAA) sparked debates on their impact, with concerns about potential exclusion and questions regarding religious discrimination. These chapters underscored the challenges of navigating security imperatives while safeguarding individual rights and promoting social harmony.

India's journey is ongoing, and the commitment to fostering dialogue, promoting inclusivity, and addressing socio-economic disparities remains paramount. The chapters explored offer glimpses into a tapestry still in the making, where individuals, communities, and leaders shape the narrative toward a future marked by unity, equality, and shared prosperity.

As India charts its course forward, the lessons learned from history, the initiatives of governance, and the global perspectives on religious harmony will guide the nation. The story of Hindu-Muslim relations in India is an evolving narrative, rich with diversity, complexities, and the potential for a shared future that transcends religious boundaries. It is a story where the chapters written today pave the way for a more inclusive and harmonious tomorrow.

Did you love *Bridging Divides: Navigating Hindu-Muslim Relations in Contemporary India*? Then you should read *Ayodhya Unveiled: A History of Faith, Struggle and Triumph*[1] by Ankush vig!

[2]

Ayodhya Unveiled: A Journey of Faith, Resilience, and Triumph" is a captivating exploration of Ayodhya's rich history and the remarkable journey leading to the construction of the Ram Mandir. Starting with the Vedic era and Lord Ram's influence, the book unravels the Mughal era's Ayodhya controversy and navigates through the post-independence landscape, delving into the transformative Ram Janmabhoomi movement.

Societal impact, Hindu-Muslim relations, and the global influence of the Ram Mandir are illuminated, providing a nuanced understanding of its significance. The narrative also addresses challenges, fostering

1. https://books2read.com/u/3kDRGG
2. https://books2read.com/u/3kDRGG

inclusivity, and envisioning future trajectories. Dedicated chapters pay homage to the Kar Sevaks, highlighting their sacrifices and contributions that shaped Ayodhya's collective consciousness.

In simple yet evocative language, this book unveils the cultural tapestry of Ayodhya, offering readers a comprehensive and insightful journey through the ages—a journey that celebrates faith, resilience, and the triumph of a nation's spirit.

Also by Ankush vig

Equity Endeavours: A Pioneering Path to Profitable Investing
Ayodhya Unveiled: A History of Faith, Struggle and Triumph
BJP Unboxed: The Story of India's Political Powerhouse
Navigating Relationships: A Guide to Healthy Choices and Happiness
Bridging Divides: Navigating Hindu-Muslim Relations in Contemporary India

About the Publisher

I am a Computer Engineer with 16 years of expertise in the IT industry. Beyond the world of technology, I am also a passionate author, channeling creativity into the written word. journey blends technical proficiency with literary flair, creating a unique and impactful professional profile.

www.ingramcontent.com/pod-product-compliance
Lightning Source LLC
LaVergne TN
LVHW091235150826
845673LV00003B/1136

* 9 7 9 8 2 1 5 9 6 5 5 7 3 *